TEACHER EDITION
(with reproduciible pages)

SONGS AND ACTIVITIES FOR LEARNING ACROSS THE CURRICULUM
BY JOHN JACOBSON

TABLE OF CONTENTS

HAL•LEONARD®
CORPORATION

7777 W. BLUEMOUND RD. P.O. BOX 13819 MILWAUKEE, WI 53213

Visit Hal Leonard Online at
www.halleonard.com

INTRODUCTION

What you learn through music you just don't forget. Music teachers and advertisers have known this for years! So why not teach every subject through one of the most effective teaching tools available to us – music? You don't need a lot of musical training to listen to an infectious song and soon have the lyrics imbedded in your memory forever. That is the purpose behind *School Fact Raps*.

In this collection, we have taken important pieces of knowledge directly from the classroom curriculum of the mid-elementary years and placed them into fun rap songs that students will enjoy learning. From the basics of how to sit at a computer or taking responsibility for protecting our world to learning the basic shapes or the terms we use to describe the herbivores and carnivores of the world, your students will be singing through their standardized tests with flying colors, and perhaps a little choreography to boot!

For each song, we have included a few teaching tips that will help make the process of teaching the rapped-fact songs more effective, and we've included some programming and staging ideas, in case you want to perform the songs. With the rap tracks (available separately – 09971270 or in a Kit – 09971342), you should have no problem learning the songs and leading your students to master them as well.

We've also provided some choreography or dance suggestions above the music itself. These are merely suggestions because more than likely your students will have a few rap move ideas of their own that we encourage you to support.

We hope you enjoy this collection and, who knows, maybe learn a thing or two along the way!

ABOUT THE WRITER

In October of 2001 President George Bush named **JOHN JACOBSON** a "Point of Light" award winner for his "dedication to providing young people involved in the arts opportunities to combine music, charitable giving and community service." John is the founder and volunteer president of America Sings! Inc., a non-profit organization that encourages young performers to use their time and talents for community service. With a bachelor's degree in Music Education from the University of Wisconsin-Madison and a Master's Degree in Liberal Studies from Georgetown University, John is recognized internationally as a creative and motivating speaker for teachers and students involved in choral music education. He is the author and composer of many musicals and choral works that have been performed by millions of children worldwide, as well as educational videos and audio recordings that have helped music educators excel in their individual teaching arenas, all published exclusively by Hal Leonard Corporation. John has staged hundreds of huge music festival ensembles in his association with Walt Disney Productions and directed productions featuring thousands of young singers including NBC's national broadcast of the Macy's Thanksgiving Day Parade, presidential inaugurations and more. John stars in children's musical and exercise DVDs, most recently the series *Jjump! A Fitness Program for Children* and is the Senior Contributing Writer for *John Jacobson's Music Express*, an educational magazine for young children published by Hal Leonard Corporation.

MATH

SHAPIN' UP SHAPES

CURRICULUM

In grade 3, students are expected to learn about basic shapes (for example, triangle), and in grade 4, they are expected to learn the names of more complicated shapes. Polygons are closed shapes made up of all straight lines. Here is a list of shapes they are generally tested on, however, rarely will they be tested on some of these higher numbers, but they are still fun to learn, especially in a rap!

- Quadrilateral (4 sides)
- Pentagon (5 sides)
- Hexagon (6 sides)
- Heptagon (7 sides)
- Octagon (8 sides)
- Nonagon (9 sides)
- Decagon (10 sides)
- Undecagon (11 sides)
- Dodecagon (12 sides)

They are also supposed to learn about three other forms (that are very hard to rhyme!):

- Pyramid: something with a polygonal base, and triangular sides that meet in a point.

- Rhombus: an oblique-angled equilateral parallelogram.

- Prism: ends that are parallel, congruent polygons and sides that are parallelograms.

TEACHING TIPS & ACTIVITIES

1. Start by teaching the students the Refrain (ms. 5-10) either by rote (in a call and response fashion) or by reading the notated rap on pages 4-6. You might also put the words on a white board, chalk board or screen that all can see and follow along.

2. Have a student write the names of the shapes on a sheet of paper, and then cut these names into strips (one shape per strip) and place them in a bowl.

3. Have the students divide into equal groups. One person from each group will draw a shape name from the bowl. That group will then make that shape out of paper, tag board or some other material.

4. Each group will also have the responsibility to learn and perform the part of the rap song that deals with their selected shape.

5. Now perform the rap and have the students stand and chant their few lines when it is their turn. It will be easy to remember, as we start with the simplest forms and go to the many-sided forms in order. During the Refrain, the entire class can stand and dance around with their shapes.

6. Once you have performed the song a couple of times, the entire class will be able to sing all of the parts with ease and expression. Then you can have the ones who hold each shape, step forward or hold up their shape when it is referred to in the song, with everybody providing the rap.

7. On a later day, have students complete "Name That Shape" activity on page 7. See Answer Key on page 40.

SHAPIN' UP SHAPES
(Math)

(4 measures introduction on recording)

Words and Music by JOHN JACOBSON

Geometrically! (♩ = 138)

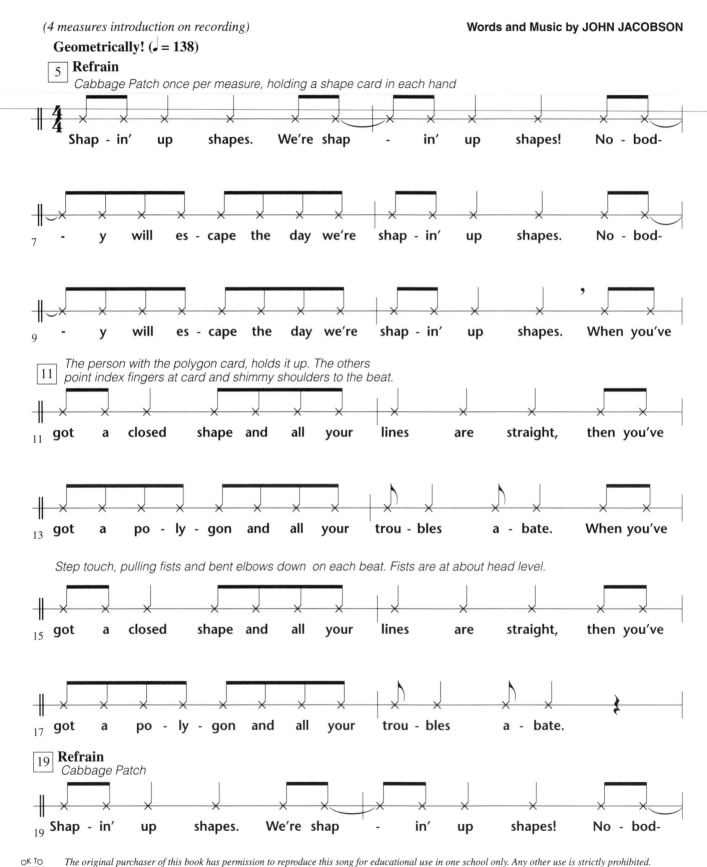

Refrain
Cabbage Patch once per measure, holding a shape card in each hand

Shap-in' up shapes. We're shap-in' up shapes! No-bod-y will es-cape the day we're shap-in' up shapes. No-bod-y will es-cape the day we're shap-in' up shapes. When you've

The person with the polygon card, holds it up. The others point index fingers at card and shimmy shoulders to the beat.

got a closed shape and all your lines are straight, then you've got a po-ly-gon and all your trou-bles a-bate. When you've

Step touch, pulling fists and bent elbows down on each beat. Fists are at about head level.

got a closed shape and all your lines are straight, then you've got a po-ly-gon and all your trou-bles a-bate.

Refrain
Cabbage Patch

Shap-in' up shapes. We're shap-in' up shapes! No-bod-

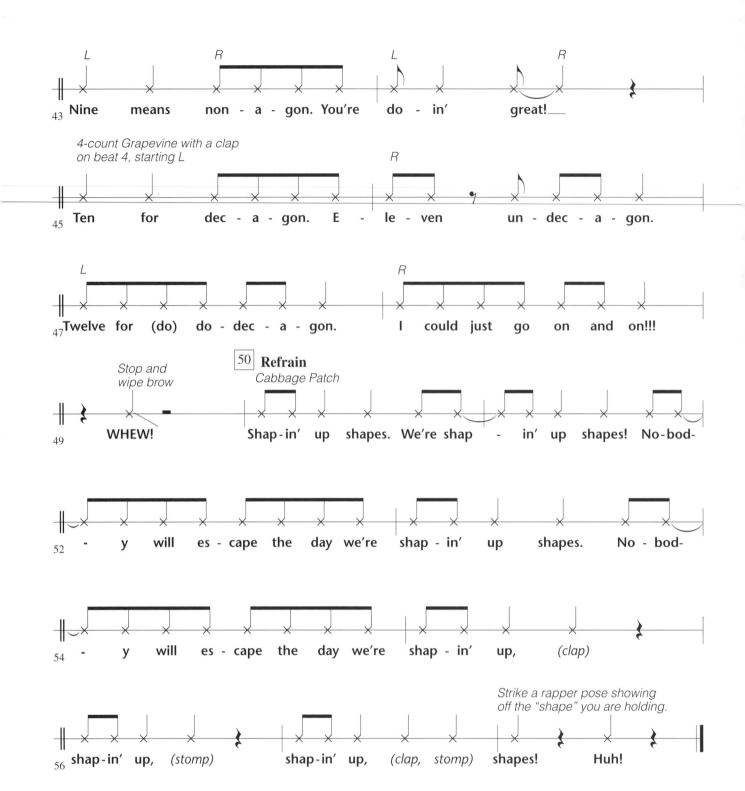

43 Nine means non - a - gon. You're do - in' great!___

*4-count Grapevine with a clap
on beat 4, starting L*

45 Ten for dec - a - gon. E - le - ven un - dec - a - gon.

47 Twelve for (do) do - dec - a - gon. I could just go on and on!!!

*Stop and
wipe brow*

50 Refrain
Cabbage Patch

49 WHEW! Shap - in' up shapes. We're shap - in' up shapes! No - bod-

52 - y will es - cape the day we're shap - in' up shapes. No - bod-

54 - y will es - cape the day we're shap - in' up, (clap)

*Strike a rapper pose showing
off the "shape" you are holding.*

56 shap - in' up, (stomp) shap - in' up, (clap, stomp) shapes! Huh!

Name That Shape!

Name _____ **Grade** _____

DIRECTIONS: Fill in the name of the shape on the line provided below each shape. Then locate and circle these 10 words in the word search puzzle. They can go forward, backward, in a straight line or diagonally.

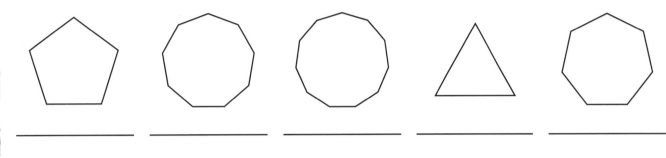

_____ _____ _____ _____ _____

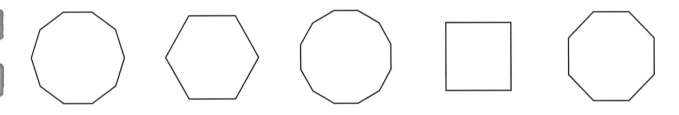

_____ _____ _____ _____ _____

```
D  X  Z  R  N  P  T  I  F  I  T  V  H  F  R  H  F  A
J  H  T  R  I  A  N  G  L  E  C  Y  B  T  O  P  N  H
M  O  W  M  Z  W  Z  A  C  T  P  S  E  Q  J  O  H  M
O  C  O  S  C  J  O  D  U  J  D  E  D  S  G  M  E  X
W  V  N  N  R  D  H  E  X  A  G  O  N  A  V  E  P  U
R  K  K  F  J  V  W  C  H  N  N  O  C  T  N  A  T  B
O  N  K  I  A  K  X  A  X  N  O  E  U  M  A  E  A  K
M  U  N  D  E  C  A  G  O  N  D  N  M  I  V  G  G  T
S  N  C  Z  Z  H  E  O  K  O  K  U  A  Z  R  G  O  S
H  F  B  B  Z  L  Y  N  D  I  N  N  X  G  E  P  N  N
Y  B  V  V  O  C  T  A  G  O  N  H  A  T  O  D  B  Z
R  Q  U  A  D  R  I  L  A  T  E  R  A  L  L  N  K  Y
```

OK TO
REPRODUCE

The original purchaser of this book has permission to reproduce this page for educational use in one school only. Any other use is strictly prohibited.

GOT SIMILE?

CURRICULUM

In third grade, or in college if you're like me, you finally master the difference between certain parts of language arts like simile and metaphor. Note, in some states and some schools, these things are taught at different grade levels and speeds, so the information can be reviewed at any time, with the undying gratitude of the classroom teacher!

- **Simile** is a figure of speech in which two things or ideas are compared – "Life is like Music" or "Music is like life."
- **Metaphor** compares two things in such a way as to imply that one is another. For example, "Life is Music" or "Music is life."

TEACHING TIPS & ACTIVITIES

1. Before learning the rap, try this activity with your students. Give them a sheet of paper, or do this as a group activity putting the examples on a board or projection. The challenge to the students is to come up with clever similes and metaphors that fit different descriptions. On one side of the paper, have students create similes from descriptions you give them. For example:

   Write a beautiful simile.
   Write a silly or funny simile.
   Write a sad simile.
   Write a simile that describes your lunch.

   On the reverse side of the page, have the students create metaphors. You could even give them a starter line and let them finish it. Such as,

   A tree is . . .   A song is . . .   My friend is . . .

2. To learn the song, have the leader teach one phrase at a time by rote, or hand out copies of the songsheet on pages 9-11.

3. Although this rap was written with simile and metaphor in mind, there are many other pieces of the language arts puzzle that could be easily reinforced through a clever rap. Once students have learned and mastered this rap, have them write new verses about other language arts subjects they are studying, but use the same Refrain (ms. 5-12).

   Some language arts concepts they are also supposed to learn about in third grade are:
   - fiction versus non-fiction.
   - the different genres of texts (such as folk tales, fables, realistic fiction); as they move onto fourth and fifth grade they'll add fantasy, historical fiction, tall tales and such.
   - story elements (main characters, setting, problem, major events, resolution, theme).

   Hand out copies of the rap worksheet on page 12. Have each student or group of students pick a new language arts subject, maybe one mentioned above or another one they are currently studying, and write a rap that explains this new concept. Fit one syllable or word to each of the rhythms in the verse. It's perfectly fine if they come up with a rap that leaves out or adds a syllable here and there, but this is a good place to start.

   When the raps are written, have students take turns performing them. Have everyone perform the Refrain from "Got Simile" in-between each new verse.

GOT SIMILE?
(Language Arts)

Words and Music by JOHN JACOBSON

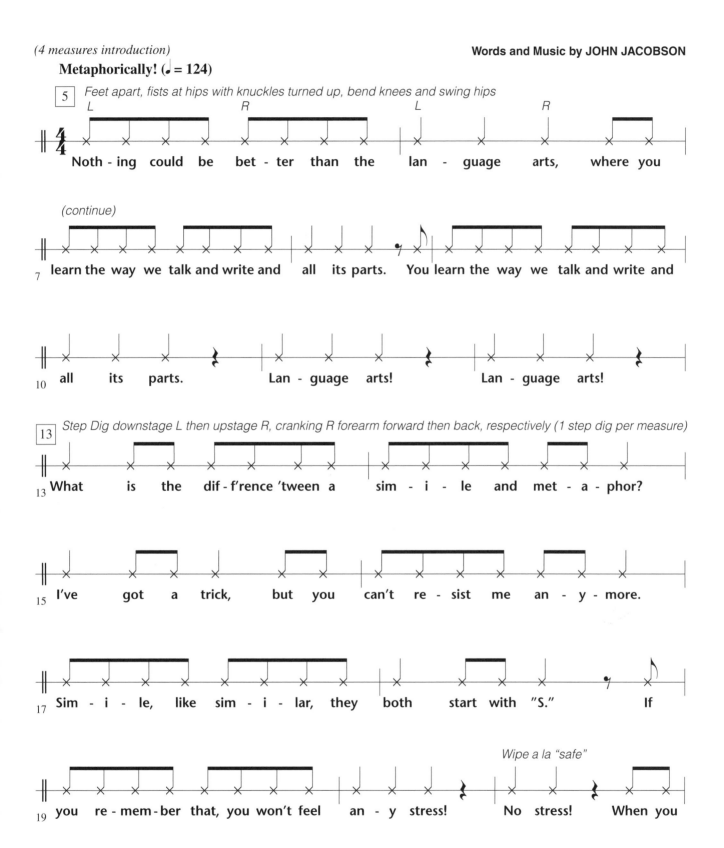

Copyright © 2009 by HAL LEONARD CORPORATION
International Copyright Secured   All Rights Reserved

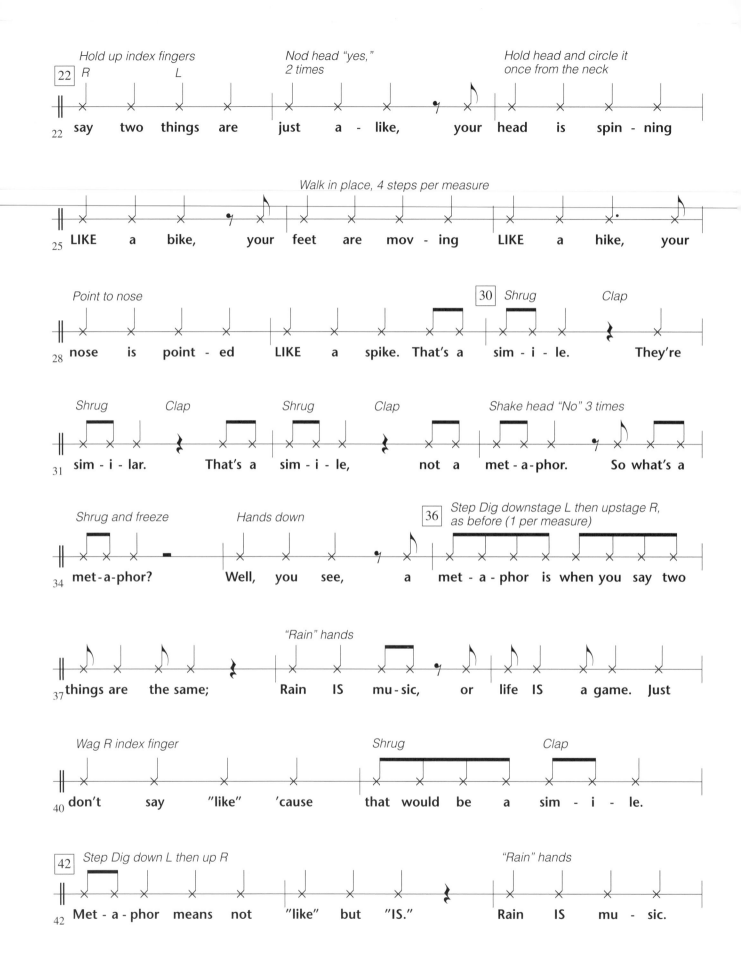

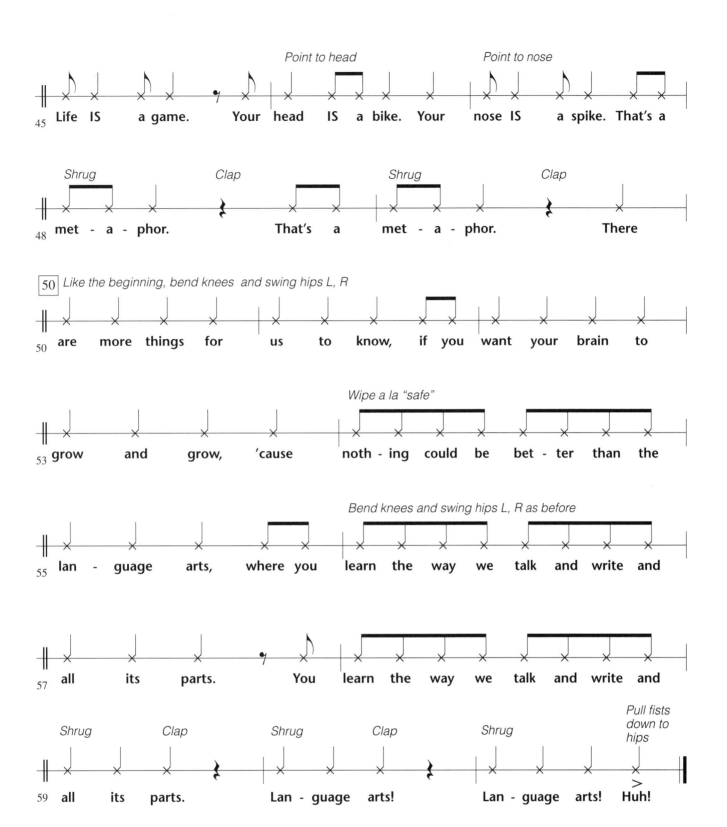

LANGUAGE ARTS ACTIVITY

____

(rap title)

DIRECTIONS: Write your own Language Arts rap. Pick a subject and write 6 short phrases about that subject. You may want to use the back of this page to jot ideas down. Then fit these words into the rap measures below by putting one syllable or word for each note.

Here is an example of a rap for different types of text:

"There are many different kinds of text,
No one is better than the next.
Like folk tales, fables and realistic fiction,
Which is hard to say without good diction.
Hard to say without good diction!
Good diction! Good diction!"

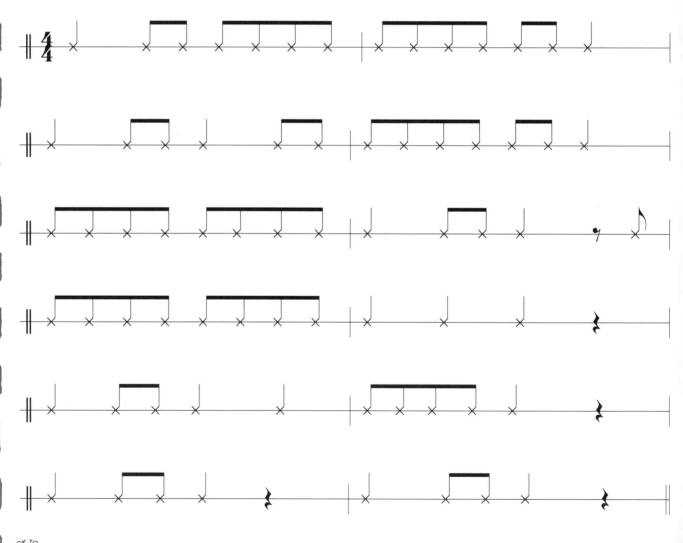

I SHARE THIS WORLD

CURRICULUM

In third grade, and reinforced in fourth and fifth, students learn the names of the seven continents – Europe, Asia, North and South America, Africa, Antarctica and Australia.

They also learn about the concept of scarcity and how it effects, or ought to, their daily lives. They learn the lesson that they can't always get everything they want. They learn they are a part of something bigger, a world full of people and animals, plants and natural resources that are meant to be shared and protected. They learn that they have a role to play as citizens of the world.

TEACHING TIPS & ACTIVITIES

1. Hold up a loaf of bread. **ASK** the students, "what is this?' Hopefully they will answer, "a loaf of bread." **SAY:** "There are a number of things that I could do with this loaf of bread. I'm thinking of four things. Can you guess what they are?" The students will begin guessing. The four answers are (although you may hear some other good ones):
   - Eat it all yourself. (If you do, then others might go hungry.)
   - Give it all away. (Nice idea, but then you might go hungry.)
   - Fight over it. (Fighting rarely solves anything, in the long run.)
   - Share it. (This is part of what it means to be a <u>citizen of the world</u>, where some things like food are scarce.)

   If you choose too, you could then actually divide the bread up between the class members and share it. Talk about what other resources are scarce, rare, fragile <u>and necessary</u>.

2. Hand out copies of the songsheet on pages 14-16, or create lyric sheets, or a projected set of either and have the students learn the rap. If you have purchased the separate CD, have students rap along with the recording. When first learning the rap, you might want to use the recorded demonstration version with the voice on the CD. Later you can use the accompaniment-only track.

3. In a performance situation, you might want to have different people take turns rapping the verses as solos. You might even have some students wear costumes representing the seven continents of the world.

4. Another fun performance idea is to have seven different groups, representing the seven continents, placed in different areas of the stage or room. They could each have a sign on a pole naming their continent and wear appropriate costuming. As the rap progresses, these seven groups could come together and even mingle to show that we are all together in this effort to create a harmonious, cared-for world, where scarcity is acknowledged and shared responsibility is embraced and celebrated.

5. At a later date, review song and complete activity on page 17. See Answer Key on page 40.

I SHARE THIS WORLD
(Social Studies)

(4 measures introduction)

Words and Music by JOHN JACOBSON

Globally! (♩ = 92)

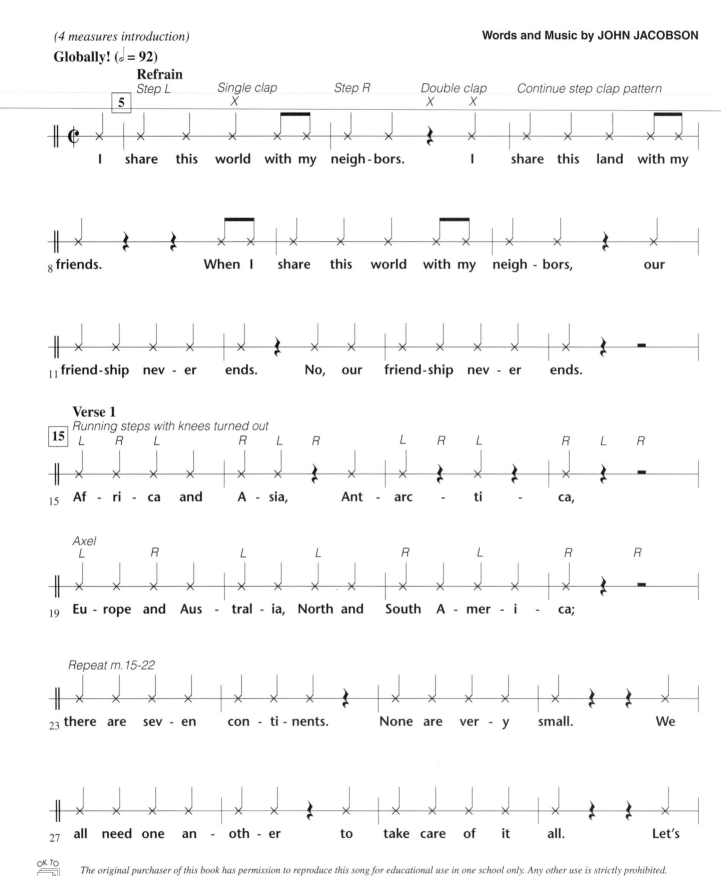

Fun With the 7 Continents

Name _____ **Grade** _____

DIRECTIONS: Each scrambled word is a name of one of the 7 continents. Unscramble each word and fill in the blank to the right with the name of the continent. Then match each continent with its rhythmic notation below by writing the number of the continent to the left of its corresponding rhythm. The first one has been done for you.

RUPEEO   1. _Europe_____

CAFIAR   2. _____

RHONT EIACMRA 3. _____

IAAS   4. _____

RNIAACATCT 5. _____

LITASUARA   6. _____

USTOH RACEIMA 7. _____

TELL ME WHAT YOU LIKE TO EAT

CURRICULUM

In grade 3, or even earlier, students often learn about the food chain. By grade 4, they are also learning about producers and consumers of food and the related terminology. What could be more fun than rapping out a song about herbivores (those who eat plants), carnivores (meat eaters), omnivores (those who eat plants and animals) and decomposers (those who eat dead things, both plants and animals)?

TEACHING TIPS & ACTIVITIES

1. Have the students as individuals, in small groups or even as an entire class, go through old magazines and cut out pictures to make collages for each of the categories: carnivore, herbivore and omnivore. Before you glue the pictures to a piece of tag board or pin them to a bulletin board, have the students tell a sentence or two about a picture they have cut out and explain what that beast eats.

2. To learn the song, have the leader teach one phrase at a time by rote, or hand out copies of the songsheet on pages 19-20.

3. Once the basic song is learned, have the students make up a one-verse rap about one of the "eaters" they cut out from a magazine – what that specific animal likes to eat, where it lives, if it is still inexistence and so on. The other students could try and guess what animal they are talking about. An example might be:

   I'm a giant carnivore,
   I sometimes swim and sometimes roar.
   I like the bitter polar air.
   I have a coat of pure white hair.
   I eat a lot of seal and fish,
   And salmon is my favorite dish.
   I'm a carnivore.
   Yeah, I'm a carnivore.

   Then the class would stop and guess what he or she is. (a polar bear) While the next rapper comes to the front of the room, the others rap the refrain (ms. 5-12): "Hey, you! You're so sweet . . . "

4. At a later date, hand out copies of the crossword puzzle on page 21, and have students complete. NOTE: it also includes the three forms of matter that are a part of 3rd Grade science curriculum. See Answer Key on page 40.

TELL ME WHAT YOU LIKE TO EAT
(Science)

(4 measures introduction)

Words and Music by JOHN JACOBSON

Gastronomical! ($\quad$ = 126)

5 *With feet apart, bounce down on each beat. On "three and," bring feet together quickly and then apart again and resume bouncing. Do this for 6 measures.*

Hey, you! You're so sweet. Tell me what you like to eat. Come on, let me know the score:

8 Herb-i-vore or carn-i-vore. If you say you like it all, om-ni-vore is what I'll call

Point R hand downstage R while push stepping R foot out to R. Then point L hand downstage L while push stepping L foot out to side.

Repeat m. 11

13 *Repeat bounce from M. 5-12*

11 you! Yeah, you! Hey, you! You're so sweet.

14 Tell me what you like to eat. If you like to eat just plants, would-n't touch a flea or ant,

17 like your grass or leaf-y leaves, then it leads me to be-lieve, a herb-i-vore. Yeah, you're a

Clap on rests

20 herb-i-vore. You eat plants! Just plants! Now

23 *Rub stomach and plié 2 times*   *Wipe "scissors" hands 4 times*   *Funky Chicken*

23 if you'd rath-er have a steak and nev-er touch a choc-'late cake, chick-en breast would do you fine, then

You Are What You Eat and More!
Science Fun Facts

Name _____ **Grade** _____

DIRECTIONS: Here's a little crossword puzzle to help review the facts. Complete the puzzle from the clues below.

ACROSS

2. I am no longer considered a major planet.

4. I am the smallest unit of living matter.

5. I eat dead things.

8. The Earth orbits around the _____.

9. I am one of three forms of matter. Granite is one.

11. I eat plants.

DOWN

1. I am one of three forms of matter. Water is one.

3. I am one of three forms of matter. Oxygen is one.

4. I eat meat.

6. The moon orbits around the _____.

7. I eat plants and meat.

10. We are all a part of the circle of _____.

COMPUTER POSTURE

CURRICULUM

Beginning in third grade and reinforced through fifth and beyond, students are to be taught the proper posture they should use when working at their computer. These are lifelong skills that will protect both their physical and mental well being.

The basic rules are:
- Eyes level with the text on the monitor
- Shoulders down, arms relaxed
- Feet and lower back supported
- Elbows level with keyboard
- Wrists slightly elevated
- Fingers curved

TEACHING TIPS & ACTIVITIES

1. To learn the song, hand out copies of the songsheet (pages 23-24), or have the leader teach one phrase at a time by rote in a call and response fashion. The students should be seated either at a real computer or at their desk or chair, pretending as though they are in front of a computer. This rap will be particularly easy to remember since the students will be literally acting out the words as they rap them.

2. Begin by rapping the first two lines of the song. Give it a lot of attitude!

   "How you gonna sit at your computer? Tell me, how you gonna sit at your computer?"

   Now ask the students to repeat those phrases, just as you spoke them – with attitude and energy!

3. Continue teaching the next 4 phrases by rote (ms. 9-16), a bit under tempo. Encourage the students to say and do what the song suggests.

4. Now, go back to the beginning and have everyone say and do verse one all together.

5. Continue to learn the rest of the song by adding only a line or two at a time in the call and response fashion, and then go back to the very beginning and speed up the tempo a bit with each repeat.

6. The students will pick this song up very quickly and you can use it every time you are going to use the computer with your class, as a reminder of the good habits they ought to develop and remember for a lifetime. You should also try to get their other classroom teachers to learn the song. Since computers are used in so many parts of their lives, these students will have plenty of opportunities to sing the song and reinforce the lesson it teaches. NOTE: It's okay if the students think it's all a little corny, they'll remember it, corny or not, and will sing it to their own children when they are older, just as we sing "Buckle Up for Safety" or "The Alphabet Song." Just have fun with it. "It feels good!"

7. At a later date, review song and complete activity on page 25. See Answer Key on page 40.

COMPUTER POSTURE
(Technology)

(4 measures introduction)

Words and Music by JOHN JACOBSON

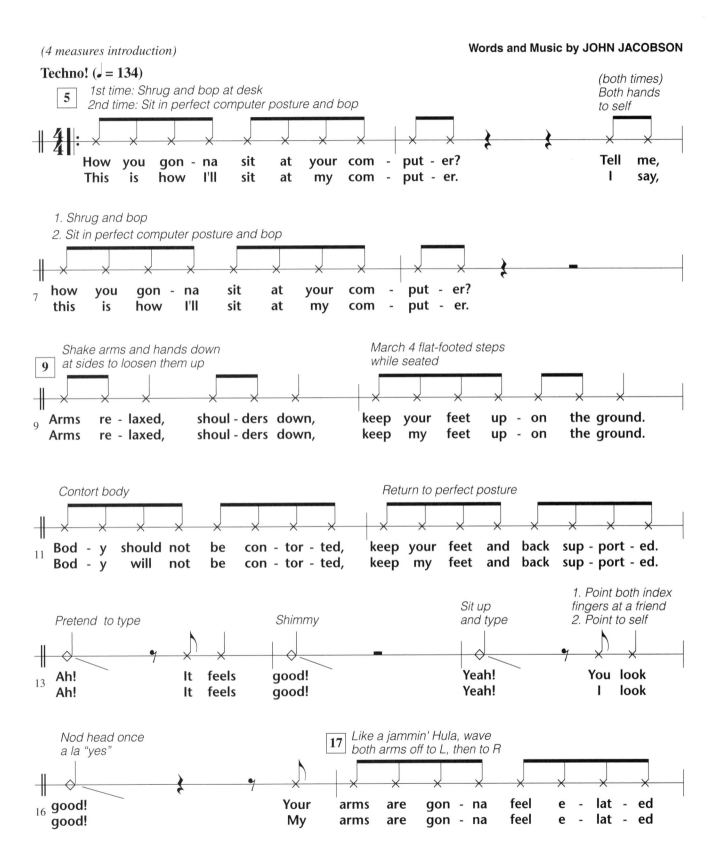

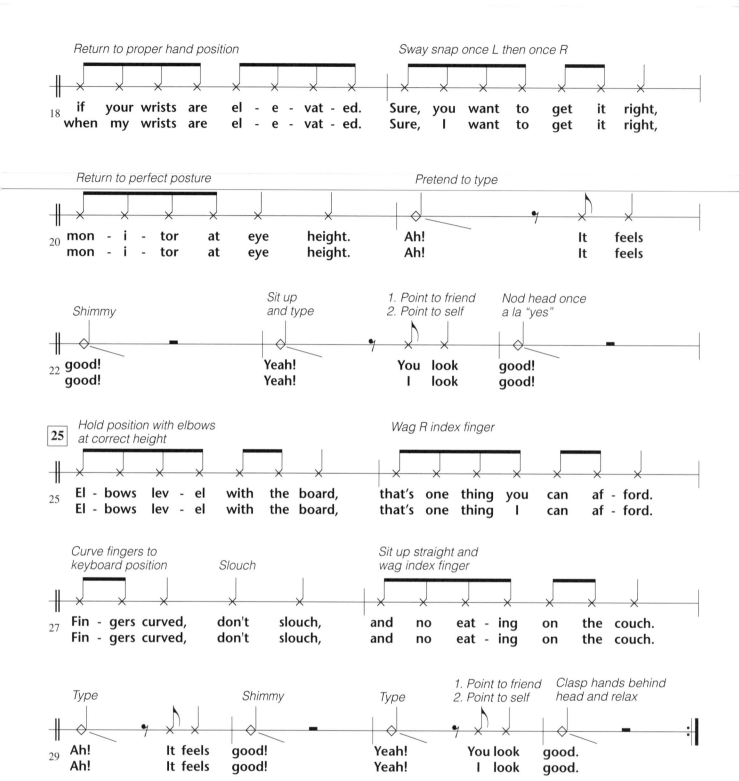

Match 'Em Up

Name _____ **Grade** _____

DIRECTIONS: Match each technology vocabulary word on the left with its correct definition on the right.

keyboard   picture that stands for a program

toolbar   shows you where you are going to type your next letter

icon   to move down, up or side to side

enter   shortcuts to program options

highlight   key used to go down to the next line

cursor   set of keys you use when typing

save   where your fingers should be when you are typing

home row   using a software program to create typed documents

scroll   to select date by clicking and dragging over it

word processing   to keep

DIRECTIONS: Fill in the missing word to complete each posture rule.

1. Eyes level with the _____ on the monitor

2. Shoulders _____, arms relaxed

3. Feet and lower back _____

4. _____ level with keyboard

5. Wrists slightly _____

6. _____ curved

SOMETHING'S MISSING WHEN I RAP

CURRICULUM

Elementary students of music are expected to learn about the elements of music. There are differing opinions on the labels of the elements of music and even on what should be included on the list, but if the students learn the terms and concepts included in this rap, they should have a pretty good start on understanding the primary elements of this thing we call music. Elements of music in this rap include: rhythm, form, dynamics, tone, harmony, texture and meter.

TEACHING TIPS & ACTIVITIES

1. *Something's Missing When I Rap* is not meant as a slam on rap music. In fact, rap music can be a wonderful teaching tool and can even be very musical. This is just a fun way to list and learn the elements of music, perhaps with a bit stronger emphasis on melody. One could even argue that there certainly IS a melody in any rap song, because the rapper's spoken voice goes up and down in pitch just as a singer's voice does when they sing a melody. If a student challenges the notion that there is no melody in rap, say "bravo!" and encourage that discussion, realizing there may be real merit to their hypothesis. After all, we often describe a speaker as having a sing-songy voice.

2. To learn the song, have the leader teach one phrase at a time by rote, or hand out copies of the songsheet on pages 27-29.

3. After students have learned the rap, challenge them with this fun exercise. Have different students select one of the elements of music and create a rap of their own. They might choose something like timbre and write a rap such as:

   > *Timbre is the color of the music.*
   > *It goes right along with tone.*
   > *If you can tell the color of the music,*
   > *You'll find you're in the timbre zone.*
   > *Some tone is dark. Other nice and mellow.*
   > *Some might be blue. Some might be yellow.*
   > *Fuzzy, rich or clear,*
   > *In your ear, you can hear.*
   > *Yo, Timbre is the color of the music.*

4. At a later date, hand out copies of the word search puzzle on page 30, and have students complete. This should be fairly easy for your older students, but it never hurts to have these words and ideas rolling around in their heads one more time. See Answer Key on page 40.

SOMETHING'S MISSING WHEN I RAP
(Music)

(4 measures introduction)

Words and Music by JOHN JACOBSON

Cha Cha Salsa (♩ = 126)

Step clap with stutter step (ss): on the "and" of Beat 1, step again on the L foot. Then continue step clapping. Do this each measure.

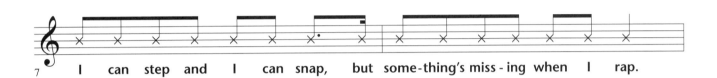

Some - thing's miss - ing when I rap. I can stomp and I can clap.

I can step and I can snap, but some-thing's miss - ing when I rap.

Some-thing's miss - ing when I rap! My mu - sic teach - er's gon - na snap. So

I put on my think - ing cap 'cause some-thing's miss - ing when I rap.

Train Step* a la Cha Cha (hip swivels)

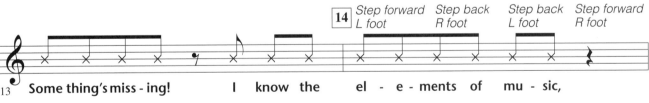

Some thing's miss - ing! I know the el - e - ments of mu - sic,

(continue)

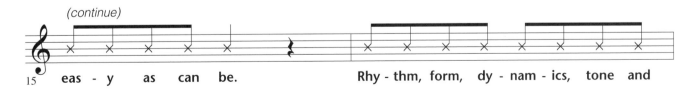

eas - y as can be. Rhy - thm, form, dy - nam - ics, tone and

* The R foot is actually stepping in same place both times.

38 *(sing)*

DO MI RE FA MI SO FA LA SO TI LA DO TI RE DO.

DO LA TI SO LA FA SO MI FA RE MI DO RE TI DO.

(back to rap)   2 claps   1 clap

Ah! That's bet - ter! Much bet - ter!

48 *Resume step claps with stutter step like the beginning*

I can stomp and I can clap. I can step and I can snap, but

some thing's miss - ing when I rap. Some-thing's miss - ing when I rap!

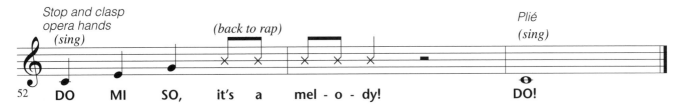

Stop and clasp
opera hands
(sing)   *(back to rap)*   *Plié*
                                          (sing)

DO MI SO, it's a mel - o - dy! DO!

On the recording, a 2-measure
vamp repeats and fades to end rap.

MUSIC ACTIVITY

It's ELEMENT-al!
Music Fun Facts

Name _____ **Grade** _____

DIRECTIONS: Locate and circle these 12 words in the word search puzzle. They can go forward, backward, in a straight line or diagonally.

```
E  N  M  I  V  N  F  Z  J  T  V  O  P  X  A  D
B  H  I  D  P  H  D  N  Y  H  N  P  W  T  S  I
N  Y  E  F  X  A  E  N  P  M  Z  T  F  T  P  J
R  H  Y  T  H  M  O  C  A  E  U  G  E  A  D  M
E  D  P  H  D  M  K  H  R  L  X  S  R  M  E  G
K  Y  B  N  R  V  E  B  H  O  L  A  I  E  P  T
A  N  Q  A  G  X  M  M  F  D  X  U  N  C  J  O
N  A  H  I  Y  I  A  M  O  Y  G  F  E  J  L  N
C  M  K  M  T  Q  B  E  R  E  W  X  H  D  O  E
N  I  O  H  R  F  R  T  M  Y  E  G  I  E  L  Q
J  C  K  D  J  R  G  E  K  T  B  U  E  B  V  K
D  S  I  I  N  S  T  R  U  M  E  N  T  S  G  G
```

DYNAMICS	MELODY	RHYTHM
FORM	METER	TEMPO
HARMONY	MUSIC	TIMBRE
INSTRUMENTS	RAP	TONE

WINNERS!

CURRICULUM

By Grade 4, it is part of the curriculum that students learn how to be good winners and good losers. I would expect that attention to good sportsmanship has been introduced long before this, but at this grade level it is formally reinforced.

Having a chant to do before and/or after a sporting event or even a classroom game might be a fun way to remind the students of proper behavior in such a realm. Teach the entire crowd at public events this rap just to remind everyone that it's a game. The lessons being taught here are that real champions are those who know how to win and lose with style and grace. Adults need to be reminded of this, too, and a rap seems a more fun way to do it, than simply sending a note home from school.

TEACHING TIPS & ACTIVITIES

1. To learn the song, have the leader teach one phrase at a time by rote, or hand out copies of the songsheet on pages 32-34.

2. There are choreography notes added above the music you can use or ignore as you see fit, but the hand shaking sequence at measure 35 should be a lot of fun. If you get to that section and want to make the rap more event-specific, you might have the students come up with new rap lyrics to fit the occasion. For instance, if you wanted to use the song for a DARE program or Drug Free rally, you might change the lyrics at the hand shake section to something like:

   Drugs bad,
   clean good
   in our
   neighborhood.
   Don't you drink
   when you drive
   if you want to stay alive.
   I can see
   you're so smart.
   Be a winner in your heart!
   Yeah! Oh Yeah!

3. I have often talked to students about one of the toughest lessons I think there is to learn in life, and that is how to be a good friend to the winner. It is relatively easy to be a good friend to someone who is having a rough time. You can allow them to cry on your shoulder. You can be sympathetic with them and in fact, it feels pretty good … for you. It isn't as easy to be a good friend to someone who seems to always win or has won something that you thought ought to go to you. When everything is going right for your friend, it can sometimes be challenging not to feel resentful and envious. This is when real character is tested. As a lesson to point out this to your students and cause them to analyze how good a friend they really are, you might have your students complete the simple multiple-choice exercise "Winning Friends" on page 35. It is a good follow-up to the "winners" rap, and can serve as a catalyst for a positive discussion about sportsmanship and choosing friends wisely. There are no right or wrong answers, just ideas.

WINNERS!
(Physical Education & Health)

(4 measures introduction)

Words and Music by JOHN JACOBSON

Triumphantly! (♩ = 126)

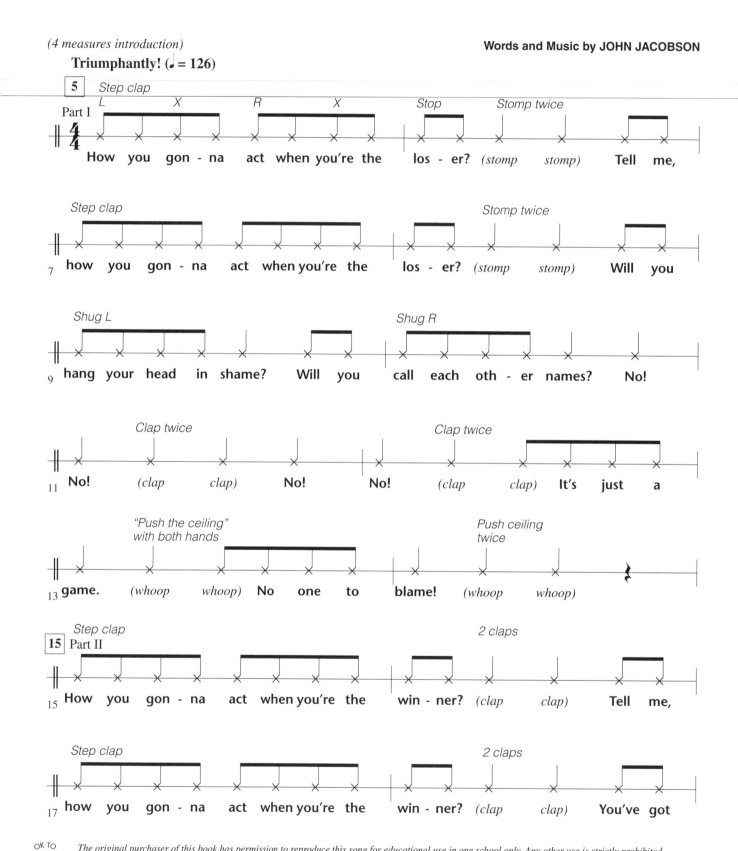

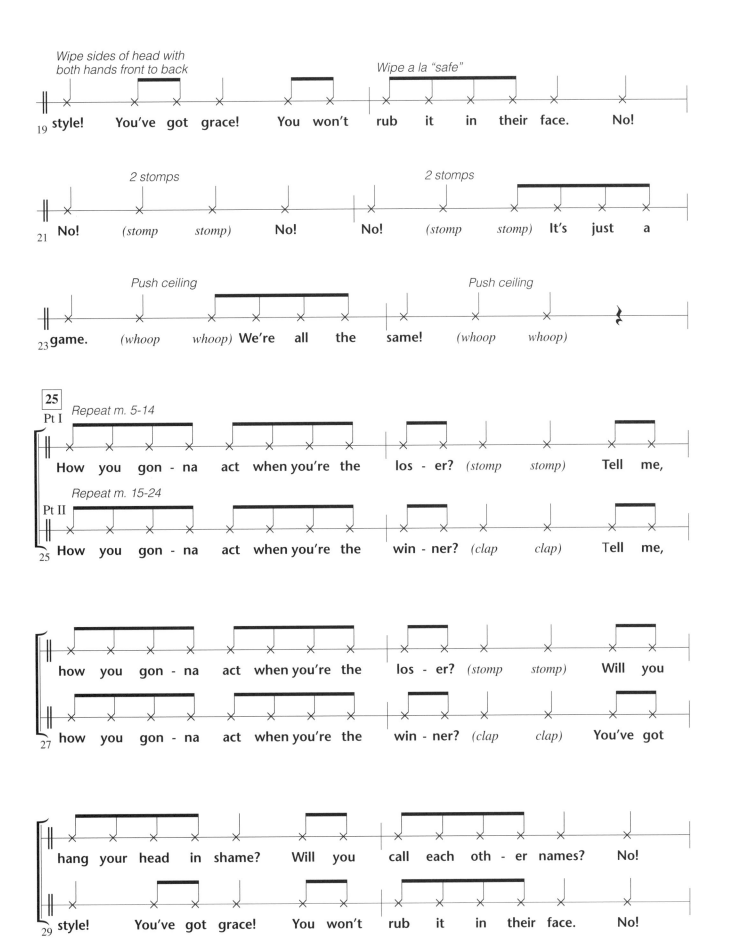

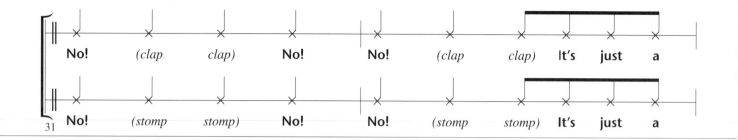

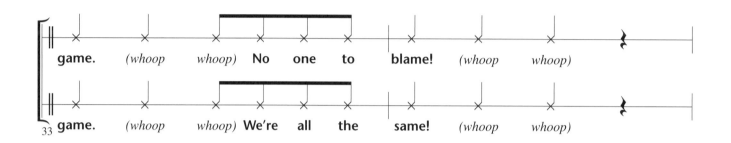

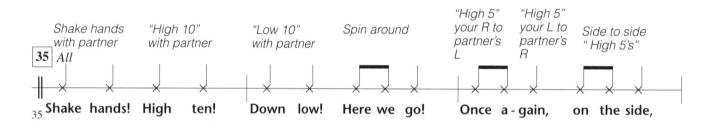

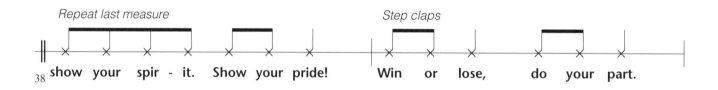

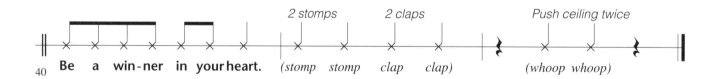

Winning Friends!

Name _____ **Grade** _____

1. When I win a game, I . . .
   a. am happy for myself and forget about my opponent.
   b. feel so bad for my opponent that I almost wish they would have won.
   c. love to gloat and rub it in. After all, that is my right as the winner.
   d. feel happy in my victory, but appreciate the good efforts of my opponents.

2. When I lose in a game, I . . .
   a. feel anger at myself.
   b. feel anger at my opponent.
   c. feel anger at the whole world.
   d. wish I would never have played the game in the first place.
   e. get over it and realize that I will have another chance another day.

3. When I win, I expect my friends to . . .
   a. want to be around me.
   b. be envious of me.
   c. congratulate me for my success and be happy for me.

4. When I lose, I expect my friends to . . .
   a. make fun of me.
   b. avoid me.
   c. support me and encourage me to try again.

5. When everything seems to go right for my friend, I . . .
   a. feel envious and angry because everything always goes right for my friend and not for me.
   b. look for ways that I can make sure everything doesn't go right for my friend.
   c. talk behind my friend's back to make me look better than my friend.
   d. feel truly happy for my friend's success. I realize that nobody always wins or loses and I know that my friend will feel the same happiness for me when it is my chance to win.

UP TO THE TEST!

Believe it or not, there are actually people in this world who enjoy taking tests! The reason is that, like anything else, you like what you are good at. Some people are very good at taking tests. The reason isn't necessarily that they are smarter than the rest of us, but most likely because they have developed some good test-taking habits that, if followed, will help anyone be a more successful test taker, with less stress and better results.

TEACHING TIPS & ACTIVITIES

1. This rap is intended to remind students of these good habits in a fun way, not just on the day of the test, but in the days and weeks leading up to it. By teaching a few "tried-and-true" lessons and reinforcing them regularly, most students will do better when the real test arrives. Most of the lyrics in this rap are there for a point of discussion. This is especially true in the repetitive refrain "Prepare! Budget! Check it out!" Go over these three ideas as you are learning the rap and discuss with the students how they pertain to good test-taking habits.

   PREPARE: Preparation for taking a test starts long before the actual testing day. It ought to include studying, completing homework assignments and reviewing study materials on a regular basis. On the day of the test, preparation should include:
   - getting a good night sleep.
   - eating a snack before test time, but not so much that it makes you groggy.
   - getting to the testing room early.
   - using the restroom ahead of time, so you don't have that to worry about.
   - not stressing because you feel stress. A little stress is normal. Just think of it as excitement and don't let it overwhelm you.

   What other kinds of tips can you think of, that will be helpful on the day of the test?

   BUDGET
   - It is very important to budget your time prior to test day. Studying regularly over a long period of time will be more effective than cramming everything in the night before.
   - Budget your time during the test so that you don't spend all of your time on one question and never get to the rest. Don't rush, but keep moving forward, keeping in mind how much time as been allowed for the task at hand.
   - What other ways can "budgeting" help you take a better test?

   CHECK IT OUT
   - Check out the whole test when you first get it.
   - Check out the easy questions first, then go back to the more challenging ones.
   - Check out your posture so that you are sitting comfortably and relaxed.
   - Check out the clock so you keep on task, but don't panic about it. Again, stay focused on the task at hand.

2. How about a whimsical test on taking a test? After having fun with this rap, have your students try the activity on page 39, "A Test on Testing", multiple-choice test in which everyone should score 100 %. Hand out copies to the students, and although they should see immediately that it is ridiculous, the one correct answer for each question could provide the opportunity to discuss, review and eventually apply good test-taking habits.

UP TO THE TEST!

Words and Music by JOHN JACOBSON

Basic Move:
Beat 1: Step out L and slap both thighs with hands.
Beat 2: Pull feet together so that you are facing downstage R and clap.
Beats 3 and 4: "Push Ceiling" – with bent elbows at shoulder height,
palms up, & upper arms parallel to the floor, push palms up on each beat.
Beats 5-8: Step out R to face front and flap Rubber legs 4 times as you lean to the R.

(4 measures introduction)

Pop Rock (♩ = 124)

5 *Basic*
We're gon-na take a test, but we will not be stressed. We

Basic
got a good night's rest, and we're gon-na do our best. Yeah, *Basic* let the test-ing start. We're

Basic
gon-na do our part. We will not fall a-part, 'cause we're real-ly ver-y smart! Pre-

13 *Hold up L index finger* *Add R index finger* *Point and accent both fingers 3 times moving them L to R* *Repeat m. 13-14*
pare! Bud-get! Check it out! Pre - pare! Bud-get!

Clap three times (2 eighths, 1 qtr.) *Wipe sides of head with both hands*
Check it out! We're cool! Piece of cake! We're

Repeat m. 17-18 **21** *March in place*
cool! Piece of cake! We all have dis - ci - pline, and

we will not give in. We know we're gon-na win, so let the fun be-gin.

Punch R fist into the air 4 times *Point R hand high to low* *Punch R fist into the air 4 times*
T! E! S! T! Full of pos-si-bil-i-ty! T! E! S! T!

A Test on Testing

Name _____ **Grade** _____

1. One of the best ways to prepare for a test is to:
   a. goof around in class.
   b. never listen to the teacher.
   c. ignore all homework assignments.
   d. study, know the work, review as you go along, ask the teacher for help when you don't understand something.

2. The night before a test, I should:
   a. stay up as late as I can and watch TV because everyone knows that your brain shrinks at night anyway.
   b. review the information that I think might be on the test.
   c. get a good night's sleep.

3. When I know it is testing day, I should:
   a. tell my mother to schedule a dental appointment at the exact time of the test.
   b. skip all meals for two days prior to the test to clear my system.
   c. eat a good breakfast and then a snack just before the test, if it is later in the day.

4. When I arrive at the testing room, I should:
   a. bring only one, dull pencil because that is all you will ever need.
   b. arrive just as the bell rings and race into the room so there is no time to get nervous.
   c. arrive early and, unless seats are assigned, choose a seat where you will not get distracted.

5. When the test is handed out, I should:
   a. complete the entire test as fast as I possibly can no matter how many wrong answers I get.
   b. spend as much time on the first question until I get it right, even if it takes the entire test period.
   c. pretend I have the flu and run from the room with my hand over my mouth.
   d. go through the test and answer the easiest questions first and then go back and work on the tougher ones.

6. When the teacher gives the directions on how to take the test, I should:
   a. ignore them and just get right at the test.
   b. never ask a question if I don't understand something about the test.
   c. listen carefully and ask a question if there is something I don't understand.

7. When the test is over, I should:
   a. worry myself silly until I find out what score I received, fasting or indulging in unlimited amounts of sweets to cleanse my system.
   b. go immediately to the textbook, find the answers to questions I was unsure of and punish myself by giving my entire allowance to the meanest kid in school.
   c. relax and reward myself by doing something I enjoy for the hard work and good effort I made on the test, regardless of how it comes out.

ANSWER KEY

PG. 7 "Name That Shape"

Fill-in-the-blank

1st row: pentagon, nonagon, undecagon, triangle, heptagon

2nd row: decagon, hexagon, dodecagon, quadrilateral, octagon

Word Search

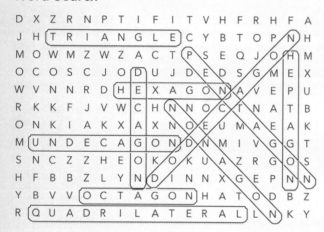

PG. 17 "Fun With the 7 Continents"

2. Africa
3. North America
4. Asia
5. Antarctica
6. Australia
7. South America

2	7
4	5
3	1
6	

PG. 21 "You Are What You Eat and More!"

Across	Down
2. pluto	1. liquid
4. cell	3. gas
5. decomposer	4. carnivore
8. sun	6. earth
9. solid	7. omnivore
11 herbivore	10. life

PG. 25 "Match 'Em Up"

Matching

keyboard – set of keys you use when typing

toolbar – shortcut to program options

icon – picture that stands for a program

enter – key used to go down to the next line

highlight – to select data by clicking and dragging over it

cursor – shows you where you are going to type your next letter

Save – to keep

home row – where your fingers should be when you are typing

scroll – to move down, up or side to side

word processing – using a software program to create typed documents

Fill-in-the-blank

1. text
2. down
3. supported
4. elbows
5. elevated
6. fingers

PG. 30 "It's ELEMENT-al!"

```
E N M I V N F Z J T V O P X A D
B H I D P H D N Y H N P W T S I
N Y E F X A E N P M Z T F T P J
R H Y T H M O C A E U G E A D M
E D P H D M K H R L X S R M E G
K Y B N R V E B H O L A I E P T
A N Q A G X M M F D X U N C J O
N A H I Y I A M O Y G F E J L N
C M K M T Q B E R E W X H D O E
N I O H R F R T M Y E G I E L Q
J C K D J R G E K T B U E B V K
D S I N S T R U M E N T S G G
```